G. Schirmer's Editions
of
Oratorios and Cantatas

ELIJAH

An Oratorio

For Full Chorus of Mixed Voices,
Soprano, Alto, Tenor, and Baritone Soli
(Double Solo Quartet of Mixed Voices)
and Piano

by

FELIX MENDELSSOHN

VOCAL SCORE

Ed. 43

ISBN 978-0-7935-4559-9

G. SCHIRMER, Inc.

DISTRIBUTED BY
HAL•LEONARD®
CORPORATION
7777 W. BLUEMOUND RD. P.O. BOX 13819 MILWAUKEE, WI 53213

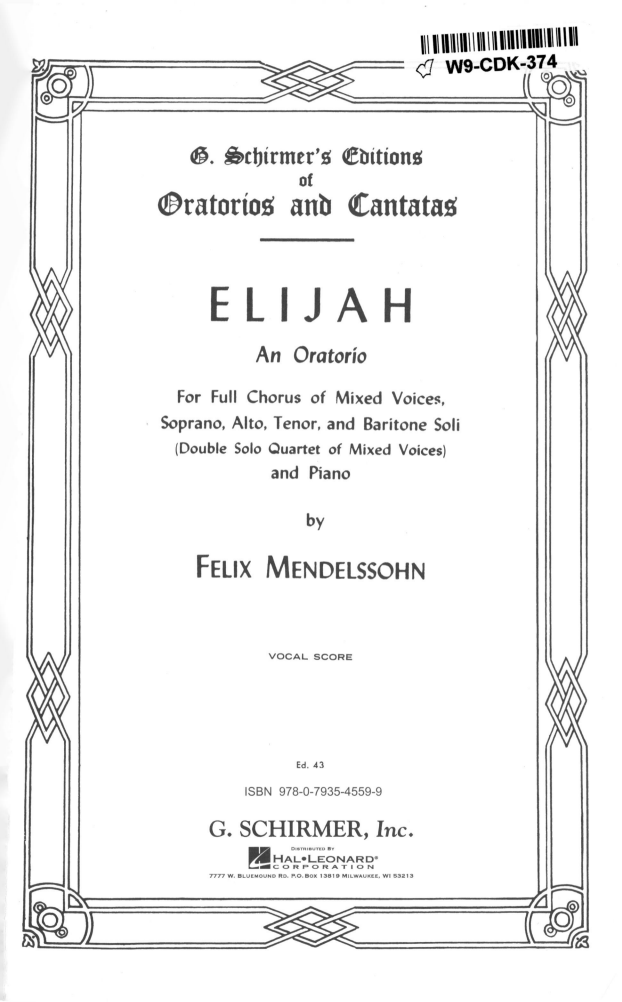

CONTENTS

PART I

PART II

ELIJAH

by

Felix Mendelssohn Bartholdy.

Introduction.

Overture.

Moderato ma poco a poco con più di fuoco. M.M. ♩ = 92.

Nº 1. "Help, Lord."

Chorus.

14

Recitative.
L'istesso tempo.

The deep affords no wa-ter,

The suckling's tongue now

And the rivers are ex-hausted!

L'istesso tempo.

cleaveth for thirst to his mouth;

The in-fant children ask for

The in-fant children ask for bread,

And there is no one break-eth it to feed them!

And there is no one.

bread.

Nº 2. "Lord, bow thine ear."
Duet, with Chorus.

Nº 3. "Ye people, rend your hearts."

Recitative.

Ye peo-ple, rend your hearts, Rend your hearts, and not your garments for your transgressions the prophet E - li-jah hath seal-ed the heavens through the word of God. I there-fore say to ye, Forsake your idols, return to God; for He is slow to anger, and mer-ci-ful, and kind, and gracious, and re-penteth Him of the e-vil.

Nº 4. "If with all your hearts."

Aria.

Nº 5. "Yet doth the Lord."

Chorus of the People.

And He vis - it - eth all the fath - ers' sins on the chil - dren

to the third and the fourth gen - e - ra - tion of them that hate

Him. His mer - cies on thou - sands fall,

№ 6. "Elijah, get thee hence."

Recitative.

№ 7. "For He shall give His angels."

Double Quartet.

No. 7A. "Now Cherith's brook."

Recitative.

(The Angel.) Alto Solo.

Now Cherith's brook is dri-ed up, E-li-jah; A-rise and depart, and get thee to Ze-repath; thither a-bide; For the Lord hath commanded __ a widow woman there to sus-

Andante.

-tain thee; And the bar-rel of meal shall not waste, neither shall the cruse of oil

Recit. **Tempo**

fail, un-til the day that the Lord sendeth rain up-on the earth. __

№ 8. "What have I to do with thee."
Solo.

And his sickness is so sore that there is no breath left in him, no

breath___ left, no breath, no breath left in him!

I go mourning all the day long, I lie down and weep at night; I

go mourning all the day long, I lie down and weep at night! See mine af _ flic _ tion,

see mine af _ flic _ tion! Be thou ___ the or _ phan's help _ _ er! be thou, be

thou the or - phan's help - - - er! _____ I go mourning all the

day long; I lie down and weep at night; See mine af -

- flic - - tion; be thou the or - phan's help - er! See _ mine af -

- flic - tion; be thou the or - phan's help - - er!

ritard.   **Elijah.**

Help my son!   There is no breath left in him! Give me thy _

Recit.

Andante sostenuto. ♩= 58.

son.

Turn unto her, O Lord, my God; Turn un-to her!

O turn in mer_cy, in mercy help this widow's son, In mer_cy

help this wi_dow's son, Lord,— in mercy help this widow's son! For Thou art

gracious, and full of com - pas_sion, And plenteous in mer_cy and truth, for Thou art

gracious, and full of com - pas_sion, And plenteous in truth and in mer - cy.

Andante con moto. *cresc.* *f*

Lord,— my God,— let the spir_it of this child re-turn, that he— a--

pp

gain may live!— Wilt thou shew won_ders, won__ders to the

dim. *pp* *sf* *dim.*

dead? There is no breath,———— no breath in him.—

sf *cresc.* *f* *pp*

Elijah.

cresc. *sempre cresc.* *f*

Lord,— my God,— let the spir_it of this child— re_turn, that he a-

p cresc.

Recit.
Widow. *sf*

_gain may live! Shall the dead a_rise, the dead a_rise and praise thee?

f **Recit.**

Recit.

Elijah.

Lord, my God, O let the spir_it of this child return, that he a _ gain may

Tempo I.

Widow.

live! The Lord hath heard thy

pray _ er; The soul of my son re _ vi _ veth, my son re _ vi _ _ _

Widow. **Recit.**

Elijah.

veth, My son re _ vi _ _ veth!

Recit.

Now be _ hold, thy son liv _ eth!

Nº 9. "Blessed are the men who fear Him."

Chorus.

peace,____ they ev-er walk in the ways of
péace, p they ev-er walk in the ways of peace,____ they
peace,____ they ev-er walk in the ways of peace,____they ev-er
peace, they ev-er walk in the ways of

peace, they walk in the ways of peace, they ev-er
ev - - er walk _____ in the ways of peace, they ev-er
walk in the ways _____ of peace, they ev-er walk _____
peace, in the ways _____ of peace, ev - _ er

walk in the ways of peace. Through dark _ ness
walk in the ways of peace.
in the ways of peace.
walk in the ways of peace.

Nº 10. "As God the Lord of Sabaoth."

Recitative with Chorus.

58

Chorus.

And then we shall see whose God is Lord.

And then we shall see whose God is God the Lord.

And then we shall see whose God is God the Lord.

Lord. And then we shall see whose God is God the Lord.

cre - scen - do

Elijah. **Recit.** **Maestoso.** ♩=80.

Rise then, ye priests of Baal; Se-lect and slay a bul-lock, and put no fire

under it; Up-lift your voi-ces and call the god ye worship; and I then will call on the Lord Je-

Allegro vivace. ♩=92.

ho-vah: And the God, who by fire shall

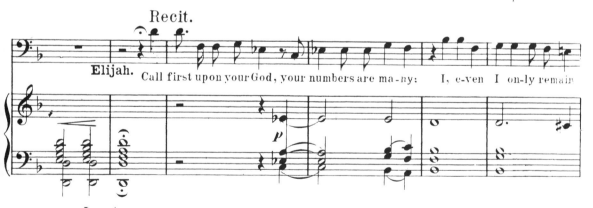

Nº 11. "Baal, we cry to thee."

Chorus.

foe. _____

Baal, let thy flames fall _____

foe. _____

Baal, let thy flames fall _____

_ and ex - tir-pate the foe! _____ Hear us. Baal!

_ and ex - tir-pate the foe! _____ Hear us. Baal!

cresc.

Hear us, Baal! hear migh-ty God!

hear, migh-ty God!

Hear us, Baal! hear migh-ty God!

hear, migh-ty God!

Nº 12. "Call him louder!"
Recitative.

Elijah. Call him loud-er! for he is a God. He talk-eth; or, he is pur-su-ing; or, he is in a jour-ney; or, per-ad-venture, he sleepeth; so a-wak-en him. Call him loud-er, call him loud-er!

Chorus. Allegro vivace. ♩ = 160.

Hear our cry, O Baal! Hear our

Nᵒ 13. "Call him louder!"

Recitative.

Elijah.

Call him louder! he heareth not. With knives and lancets cut yourselves af-ter your manner;

Allegro molto. ♩ = 160.

Leap up-on the al - tar ye have made;

Call him, and prophesy; Not a voice will answer you, none will listen; none heed you.

Chorus.
Presto. ♩. = 126.

Baal!

Baal!

Baal!

Baal!

Presto.

Baal!

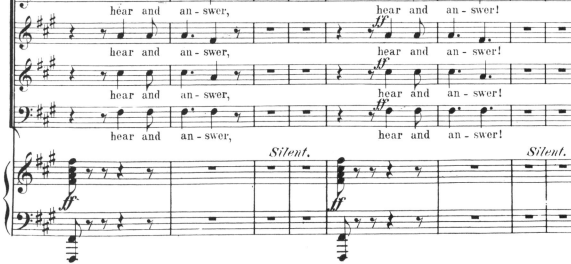

Nº 14. "Draw near, all ye people."
Recitative and Air.

Lord, and an-swer me, O hear me, Lord, and answer me! Lord God of A-braham,

I-saac and Is-ra-el; O hear me, O hear me and an-swer me; and shew this peo-ple that

Thou art Lord God; and let their hearts a-gain be turn-ed; O shew this peo--ple that

Thou art Lord God, and let their hearts a-gain be turn-ed, Lord;

and let their hearts, and let their hearts again be turn-ed!

Attacca subito.

№ 15. "Cast thy burden upon the Lord."

Choral.

No 16. "O Thou, who makest thine angels spirits."
Recitative.

Chorus.

Allegro con fuoco. ♩ = 152.

Recit.
Elijah.

Take all the prophets of Baal, and let not one of them es-cape you.

Recit.

Bring them down to Kishon's brook; and there let them be slain.

Tempo.

Take all the prophets of

Take all the prophets of

Take all the prophets of

Tempo. Take all the prophets of

Baal; and let not one of them es-cape us; bring all, and slay them!

Baal; and let not one of them es-cape us; bring all, and slay them!

Baal; and let not one of them es-cape us; bring all, and slay them!

Baal; and let not one of them es-cape us; bring all, and slay them!

Nº 17 "Is not His word like a fire?"
Aria.

rock. His word is like a fire, and like a

ham - - mer, A ham - - mer that break - eth the

rock. For God is an - - gry,

an - gry with the wicked ev - ry day, for God is an - gry with the

wicked every day; and if the wicked turn not, the Lord will whet his

sword, will whet his sword; and He hath bent his

bow, and made it read - y, and made it

read - y, read - - y! Is not His

word ___ like a fire? and like a

ham - mer that break - eth the rock, and like a ham - mer that break - eth the

rock? Is not His word _____ like a fire, and like a

ham - - mer, a ham - - mer that break - eth the

rock? that break - eth the rock, that break - eth the

rock; and like a fire, ___ like a ham - - mer, that

break - eth the rock; is not His word like a

ham - - mer that break - - eth the rock, is not His

word like a ham - - mer that break - - eth

_ the rock in-to pie - - ces,

Più lento.

Is not His word— like a ham mer that break - eth the

rock?

Tempo I.

№ 18. "Woe unto them who forsake Him!"

Arioso.

fled; Though they are by Him re - deem - ed: even from Him they have fled. Woe

unto them! Woe un - - to them!

No. 19. "O man of God, help thy people!"

Recitative.

Recit.

Obadiah.

O man of God, help thy peo - ple! A - mong the

IANO.

idols of the Gentiles, are there any that can command the rain, Or cause the heav'ns to give their

show - ers? The Lord our God a - lone can do these things.

Nº 19A. "Thou hast overthrown thine enemies!"

Recitative and Chorus.

Nº 20. "Thanks be to God!"

SECOND PART.

№ 21. Hear ye, Israel!

Aria.

I, I am He that com-fort-eth, be not a-fraid, be not a-fraid; for

I am thy God, I will strength-en thee! I

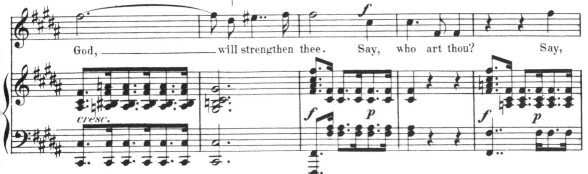

the Lord, will strengthen thee; for I, thy

God, will strengthen thee. Say, who art thou? Say,

who art thou, that thou art a-fraid of a man that shall die;

and for-get-test the Lord, the Lord thy Ma - ker, —

—who hath stretch - ed forth the hea - - - vens,

and laid the earth's foun - da - tions, the earth's foun -

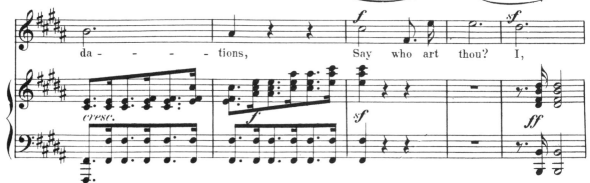

da - - - tions, Say who art thou? I,

I am He that com - fort - eth; Be not a - fraid, be not a-

fraid ———— for I, I am thy God; Be not a-

fraid, Be not a-fraid, I I

am thy God; Be not a-fraid, be not a-

fraid, for I, thy God ———— will

strength-en thee."

Nº 22. "Be not afraid."

Chorus.

From Mendelssohn's "Elijah"

fraid, thy help is near, Be not a-fraid, for He is near; be not a-

He is near; Be not a-fraid, thy help is near, be not a-fraid.____

Be not a-fraid, for He is near; Be not a-fraid, thy help is near;____

Be not a-fraid, Be not a-fraid.

fraid, be not a-fraid thy help is near. Be not a-fraid!

thy help is near. Be not a-fraid!

be not a-fraid, thy help is near. Be not a-fraid!

be not a-fraid, thy help is near. Be not a-fraid!

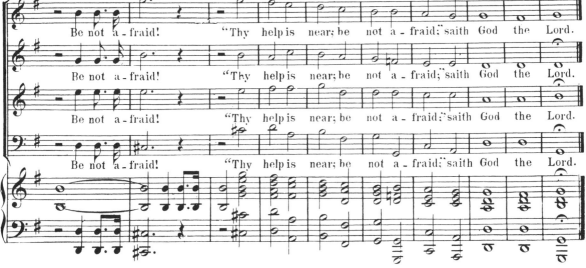

Be not a-fraid! "Thy help is near; be not a-fraid," saith God the Lord.

Be not a-fraid! "Thy help is near; be not a-fraid," saith God the Lord.

Be not a-fraid! "Thy help is near; be not a-fraid," saith God the Lord.

Be not a-fraid! "Thy help is near; be not a-fraid," saith God the Lord.

Nº 23. "The Lord hath exalted thee."

Recitative and Chorus.

Thou hast killed the righteous, and al-so taken possession.

And the Lord shall smite all Is-rael as a reed is shaken in the wa-ter; and He shall give Is-ra-el up, And thou shalt know He is the Lord.

The Queen.

Have ye not heard, heard he hath pro-phesied a-gainst all Is-ra-el?

We

forth and seize E-li-jah, for he is worthy to die; slaughter him! do unto him— as he hath done.

№ 24. "Woe to him."

Chorus.

Nº 25. "Man of God."

Recitative.

Andante sostenuto. ♩ = 63.

Lord thy God doth go, doth go with thee: He will not fail thee, He will not for-sake thee. Now be-gone, be-gone, and bless me;

Now be-gone, and bless me al-so.

Elijah.

Recit.

Though strick-en they have not grieved! Tarry

here, my ser-vant, the Lord be with thee. I jour-ney hence to the

Adagio. ♩ = 66.

wil-der-ness.

Attacca:

Nº 26. "It is enough."
Aria.

ter than my fa—thers, I am not bet—ter, I am not bet—ter than my

fa———thers!

I de—sire——— to live no long—er; now let me

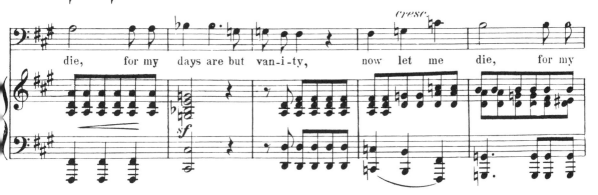

die, for my days are but van-i-ty, now let me die, for my

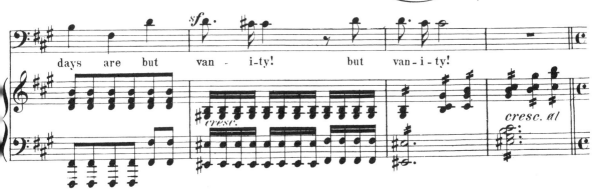

days are but van-i-ty! but van-i-ty!

136

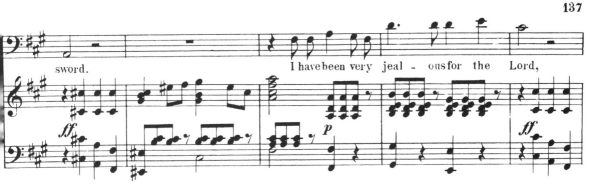

sword.   I have been very jeal - ous for the Lord,

for the Lord God of Hosts, very jealous for the

Lord,   the Lord God of Hosts, and I, e-ven I   on-ly am left;—

and they seek my life,   and they seek my life   to   take

it,   to   take   it   a - way.

Adagio. ♩ = 66.

con forza
dim.

It is e - nough! It is e - nough!

It is e - nough. O Lord! now take away my life,___ for I am not

bet - ter than my fa - thers; now let me die,

Lord,___ take a - way my life!

Nº 27. "See, now he sleepeth."
Recitative.

Recit.

Tenor Solo.

See, now he sleep - eth beneath a ju-ni-per tree in the wil-derness! and there the

PIANO.

No. 28. "Lift thine eyes."

Trio

He hath said, thy foot _____ shall not be mov-ed. Thy Keeper will ne-ver

He hath said, thy foot shall not be mov-ed. Thy

He hath said, thy foot shall not be mov-ed. Thy

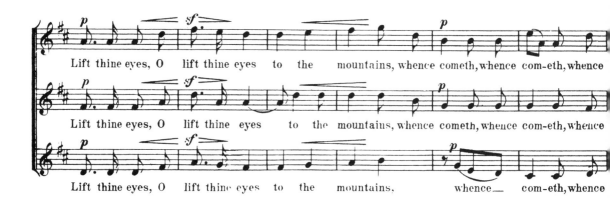

slum - ber, never, will never slum - ber, never slum - - - ber.

Keeper will never slum - ber, nev-er, will never slum - - - ber.

Keeper will never slum - ber, nev-er, will never slum-ber, will ne - ver slum - ber.

Lift thine eyes, O lift thine eyes to the mountains, whence cometh, whence com-eth, whence

Lift thine eyes, O lift thine eyes to the mountains, whence cometh, whence com-eth, whence

Lift thine eyes, O lift thine eyes to the mountains, whence___ com-eth, whence

com - eth help, whence com-eth, whence com-eth, whence com-eth help.

com - eth help, whence com - - eth, whence com-eth, whence com-eth help.

com - eth help, whence com - - eth, whence com-eth, whence com-eth help.

№ 29. "He, watching over Israel."

Chorus

No. 30. "Arise, Elijah."

Recitative.

Nº 31. "O rest in the Lord."
Aria.

Him. wait pa-tient-ly for Him; O rest in the Lord; wait pa-tient-ly for

Him, and He shall give thee thy heart's de - sires, and He shall

give thee thy heart's de - sires, and He shall give thee thy heart's de -

sires. O rest in the Lord, O rest in the Lord, and wait,

wait pa - tient - ly for Him.

№ 32. "He that shall endure."

Chorus.

№ 33. "Night falleth round me."

Recitative.

Elijah. Night falleth round me, O Lord! Be Thou not far from me! hide not Thy face, O Lord, from me; My soul is thirsting for Thee, as a thirsty land.

Soprano Solo. (The Angel.) A - rise, now! get thee without! stand on the mount before the Lord: for there His glo-ry will ap - pear, ____ and shine on thee!

Thy face must be veil-ed, for He draweth near.

Nº 34. "Behold, God the Lord."

Chorus.

But yet the Lord was not in the earth - - quake.

But yet the Lord was not in the earth - quake.

But yet the Lord was not in the earth - - quake.

But yet the Lord was not in the earth - - quake.

And af - ter the earth-quake there came a fire,— And af - ter the

And af - ter the earth-quake there came a fire, And af - ter the

And af - ter the earth-quake there came a fire, And af - ter the

And af - ter the earth-quake there came a fire, And af - ter the

earth-quake there came a fire,— the sea was up - heav - ed,

earth-quake there came a fire, the sea was up - heav - ed,

earth-quake there came a fire, the sea was up - heav - ed,

earth-quake there came a fire, the sea was up - heav - -

the earth was shak - en, _____ and af - ter the earth - - quake _____
the earth was shak - en, _____ and af - ter the earth - - quake _____
the earth was shak - en, and af - ter the
- - - ed, and af - ter the

there came a fire, and af - ter the earth - quake there
there came a fire, and af - ter the earth - quake there
earth - quake _____ there came a fire, and af - ter the
earth - - quake _____ there came a fire, and af - ter the

came _____ a _____ fire. But yet the Lord was not, But yet the
came _____ a _____ fire. But yet the Lord was not, But yet the
earth - quake a fire. But yet the Lord was not, But yet the
earth - quake a fire. But yet the Lord was not, But yet the

Lord was not in the fire, But yet the Lord was not in the fire,

Lord was not in the fire, But yet the Lord was not in the fire,

Lord was not in the fire, But yet the Lord was not in the fire,—

Lord was not in the fire, But yet the Lord was not in the fire,—

Lord was not in the fire, But yet the Lord was not in the fire,—

sempre ff

But yet the Lord was not in the fire,— But yet the Lord was not in the fire.—

But yet the Lord was not in the fire,— But yet the Lord was not in the fire.—

But yet the Lord was not in the fire,— But yet the Lord was not in the fire.—

But yet the Lord was not in the fire,— But yet the Lord was not in the fire.—

And af-ter the fire there came a still small voice _____

And af-ter the fire there came a still small voice _____

And af-ter the fire there came a still small voice _____

And af-ter the fire there came a still small voice _____

№ 35. "Holy is God the Lord."

Recitative, Quartet and Chorus.

earth; Now His glo - ry hath fill - ed all the earth; now His glo - ry hath
earth; Now His glo - ry hath fill - ed all the earth; now His glo - ry hath
earth; Now hath His glo - ry fill - ed all the earth; now His glo - ry hath
earth; Now fill - ed all the earth, fill - ed all the earth; now His glo - ry hath
earth, hath fill - ed all, hath fill - ed all the earth; now His glo - ry hath
earth, fill - ed all, hath fill - ed all the earth; now His glo - ry hath
earth, fill - ed all, hath fill - ed all the earth; now His glo - ry hath
earth, hath fill - ed, fill - ed all the earth; now His glo - ry hath
ff dim.
pp
fill - ed all the earth, fill - ed all, hath fill - ed all the
fill - ed all the earth, fill - ed all the earth, fill - ed all the
fill - ed all the earth, hath fill - ed all the earth, hath fill - ed all the
fill - ed all the earth, hath fill - ed, fill - ed all the
fill - ed all the earth, His glo - ry now hath fill - ed all the
fill - ed all the earth, His glo - ry now hath fill - ed all the
fill - ed all the earth, His glo - ry now hath fill - ed all the
fill - ed all the earth, His glo - ry hath fill - ed all the
ff dim.
pp

earth. now___ His glo - ry hat fill-ed all the earth.

earth. now___ His glo - ry hat fill-ed all the earth.

earth. now___ His glo - ry hat fill-ed all the earth.

earth, now___ His glo - ry hat fill-ed all the earth.

earth. now His glo-ry hath fill-ed all the earth. hath fill-ed all the earth.

earth, now His glo-ry hath fill - ed all the earth. hath fill-ed all the earth.

earth, now His glo-ry hath fill - ed all the earth. hath fill-ed all the earth.

earth, now His glo-ry hath fill - ed all the earth, hath fill-ed all the earth.

Nº 36. "Go, return upon thy way."
Chorus and Recitative.

A tempo, Adagio non troppo. ♩ = 63.

Soprano.

Alto.

Tenor.

Go, re-turn up-on thy way! For the Lord yet hath left him sev - en thousand in

Bass.

Go, re-turn up-on thy way! For the Lord yet hath left him sev - en thousand in

A tempo, Adagio non troppo.

PIANO.

N.º **37.** "For the mountains shall depart."

Arioso.

For the moun - tains shall de - part,____

____ and the hills,__ the hills be re - mov - - - ed; but Thy kindness shall

not de - part; but Thy kindness, Thy kind - - -

- ness shall not__ de - part_____ from me; nei - ther shall the

cov - enant of Thy peace, of Thy peace be re - mov-ed. neither

shall ____ the cov-e-nant of Thy peace ____ be re-mov-ed; but Thy

kindness shall not de-part, shall not de-part, ____ but Thy kind -

- ness shall not ____ de -part, shall not ____ de-part from

me; nei- ther shall be re -mov-ed the cov - -

- - e - nant of ____ Thy peace.

№ 38. "Then did Elijah."
Chorus.

N⁰ 39. "Then shall the righteous shine forth."

Aria.

shine in their heav'n-ly Fa-ther's realm.

No 40. "Behold, God hath sent Elijah."

Recitative.

Andante sostenuto.

Soprano Solo.

Behold, God hath sent E-li-jah the prophet, before the

PIANO.

com-ing of the great and dread-ful day of the Lord. And he shall turn the heart of the

fa-thers to the children, and the heart of the children un-to their fathers: lest the Lord shall

come and smite the earth, and smite the earth with a curse.

№ 41. "But the Lord from the north."

Chorus.

№ 42. "O come, every one that thirsteth".

Andante sostenuto. ♩=76. Quartet.

O come come ev'ry one that thirst-eth, come, O come to

thirst-eth, come to Him; come ev'ry one that thirsteth, to the

wa-ters, O come un-to Him; come ev'ry one that thirst-eth, to the

come to the wa-ters, come! O come to Him!

sf p

Him, O come to the wa — — — ters, come to Him, O come, O

cresc.

wa — — — — ters, come to Him, O come, O come

cresc.

wa — ters come, O come to Him, O come

cresc.

O come to Him, come, come to Him, O come to

fp *p*

come, O come to Him!

f *p*

—to Him, O come to Him!

f *p*

—to Him, come to Him!

f *p*

Him, O come to Him!

sf *p*

Nº 43. "And then shall your light break forth."

Chorus.